GEOLOGY ROCKS!

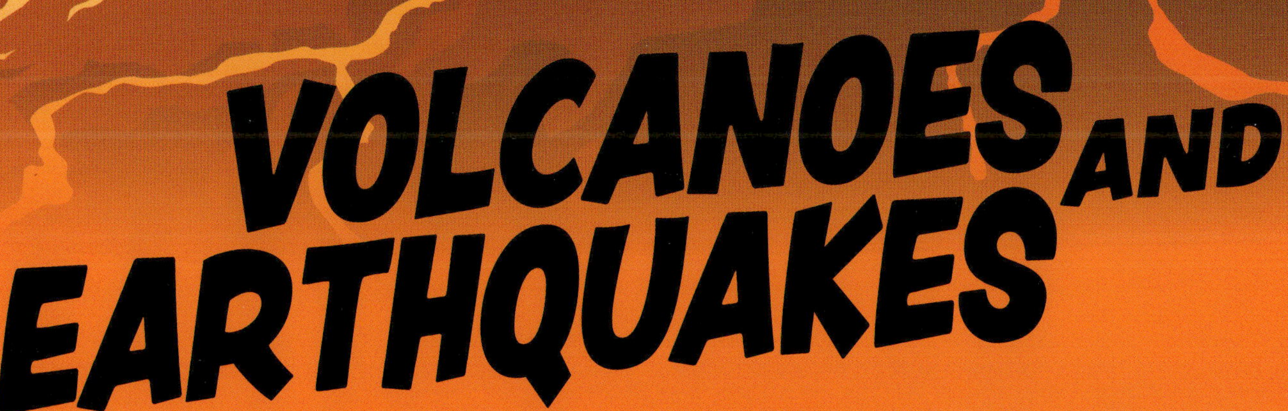

CLAUDIA MARTIN

Please visit our website, www.garethstevens.com. For a free color catalog of all our high-quality books, call toll free 1-800-542-2595 or fax 1-877-542-2596.

Published in 2025 by
Gareth Stevens Publishing
2544 Clinton St.
Buffalo, NY 14224

First published in Great Britain in 2023 by Wayland

Author and editor:
Claudia Martin

Series designer:
Rocket Design (East Anglia) Ltd

Proofreader:
Annabel Savery

Cataloging-in-Publication Data
Names: Martin, Claudia.
Title: Volcanoes and earthquakes / Claudia Martin.
Description: Buffalo, NY : Gareth Stevens Publishing, 2025. | Series: Geology rocks! | Includes glossary and index.
Identifiers: ISBN 9781538293997 (pbk.) | ISBN 9781538294000 (library bound) | ISBN 9781538294017 (ebook)
Subjects: LCSH: Volcanoes--Juvenile literature. | Volcanic eruptions--Juvenile literature. |
Classification: LCC QE521.3 M37 2025 | DDC 551.21--dc23

Picture acknowledgements: National Archives and Records Administration: H.D. Chadwick 28tr; Shutterstock: Den Zorin front cover t, 1, B illustrations front cover b, greenpic.studio back cover l, 21cr, 23tr, 27br, Designua back cover cl, 5b, 10c, 16, elenabsl back cover c, VectorMine back cover r, 6b, 8c, 22b, 24br, Virinaflora 2tr, BlueRingMedia 3tr, Jonas D Bell 3cr, 7bl, Islamic Footage 3bl, 15b, YummyBuum 3br, 10tl, 10b, CRStocker 4bc, 32bl, Peter Hermes Furian 5tr, Tartila 8b–9t, 32tr, austinding 9br, Frans Delian 11t, metamorworks 12b, ProStockStudio 13b, 31cr, Jakinnboaz 14, Valeriy Poltorak 15t, kavram 15c, Amadeu Blasco 18–19, BlackMac 19br, Kingppin 20–21, Zack Frank 20c, 27cr, Ares Jonekson 21t, Wead 23c, Antonio Salaverry 23bl, Josip Pastor 23br, Lorcel 25t, Cmitry Kovba 25b, Stephen James Burke 26cl, Javarman 26cr, redswept 26bl, Kevin Lings 26br, Angelo Cordeschi 27tl, J. Helgason 27tr, Brisbane 27cl, Moshe Einhorn 28c, Bibadash 31t; Steve Evans: 9bl, 19bl.

All additional design elements from Shutterstock or drawn by designer.

Printed in the United States of America

CPSIA compliance information: Batch #CSGS25: For further information contact Gareth Stevens at 1-800-542-2595.

BE CAREFUL!

- Wear an apron and cover surfaces.
- Tie back long hair.
- Ask an adult for help with cutting.
- Check materials for allergens.

We recommend adult supervision at all times while doing the activities in this book. Always be aware that materials may contain allergens, so check the packaging for allergens if there is a risk of an allergic reaction. Anyone with a known allergy must avoid these.

CONTENTS

Learn about eruptions on page 18!

Find out about the San Andreas Fault on page 7.

Earthquakes can trigger huge waves. Find out why on page 10.

ON THE MOVE

Moving plates of rock cause most earthquakes and volcanoes!

Around 4.5 billion years ago, Earth formed from a cloud of gas and dust that was spinning around the sun. At first, Earth was so hot it was a molten mass of rock and metal. Over millions of years, its surface cooled into solid rock and cracked into huge plates.

Look inside

Earth's core, reaches 10,800°F (6,000 °C). The core is made of metal, mostly iron and nickel. The metal in the outer core is so hot it's liquid, but in the inner core it's squeezed so tightly it's solid. Surrounding the core is the rocky mantle. With a temperature of 930 to 7,200 °F (500 to 4,000 °C), the mantle's rock is partly melted. Earth's surface of solid rock, 3 to 62 miles (5 to 100 km) thick, is called the crust.

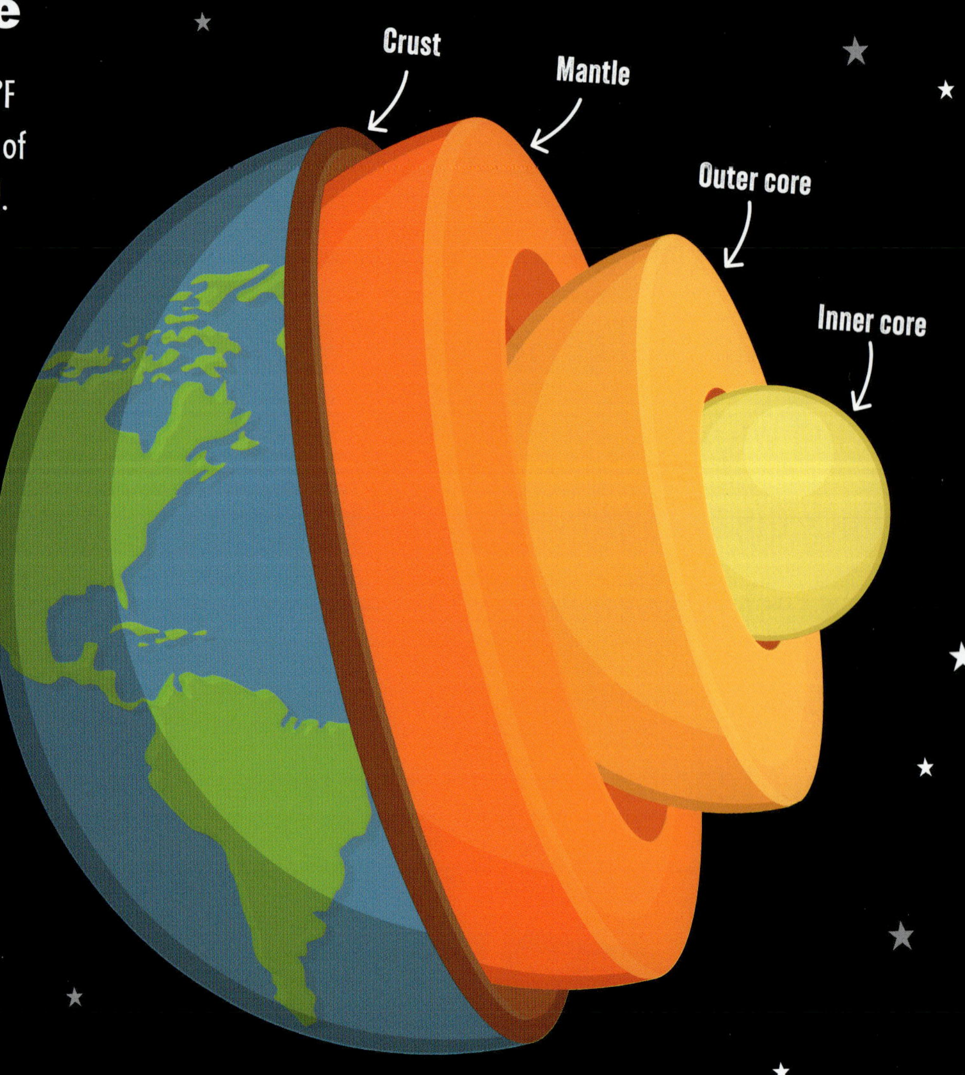

Tectonic plates

Earth's crust and upper mantle are broken into chunks called tectonic plates. There are eight large plates and lots of smaller ones. The plates move slowly, usually just 1 inch (3 cm) a year. This movement is caused by the slow flow of the mantle's hot rock.

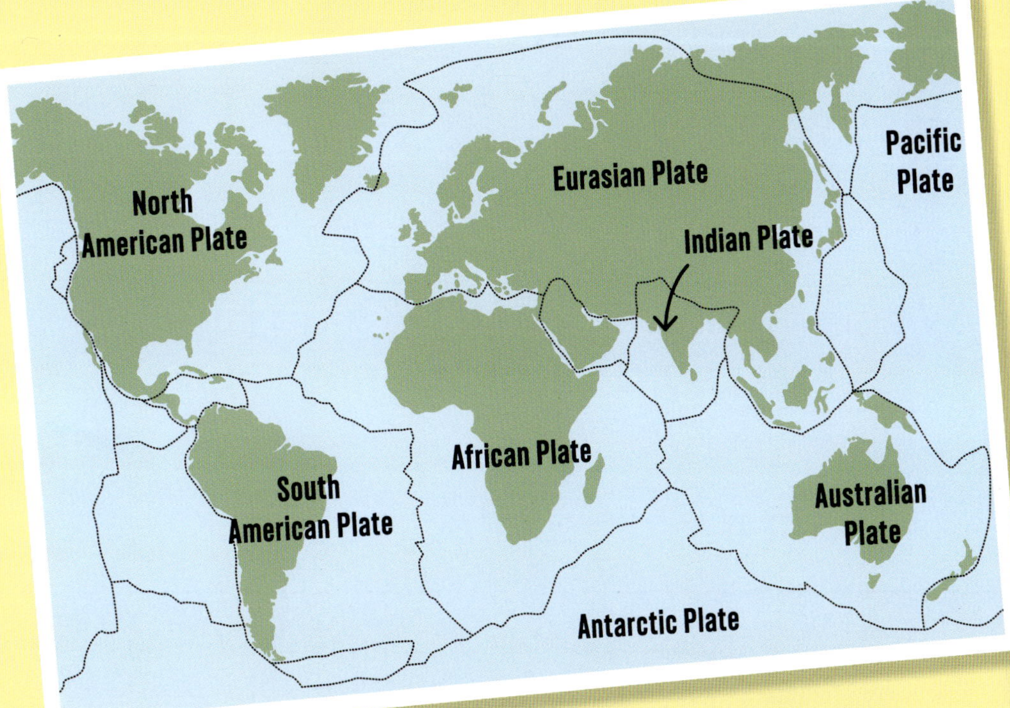

Sideways, backward, forward

Most earthquakes and volcanoes occur along the edges of plates, which are called boundaries. Some plates move towards each other, while others move apart or sideways.

QUICK QUIZ!

On average, how far do tectonic plates move every year: 1 inch (3 cm), 1 foot (30 cm), or 1 mile (1.6 km)? Answer on page 28.

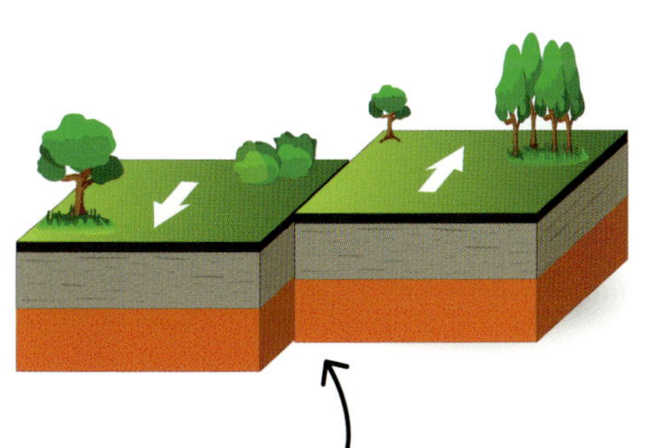

TRANSFORM BOUNDARY

Where two plates are moving past each other, earthquakes can take place.

DIVERGENT BOUNDARY

Where two plates are moving apart, earthquakes are common. Melted rock wells up, forming volcanoes.

Ouch! Hot!

CONVERGENT BOUNDARY

Where two plates are moving toward each other, melted rock is forced upwards, making volcanoes. Earthquakes can happen too.

WHAT IS AN EARTHQUAKE?

Most earthquakes are caused by rock sticking and slipping.

Earthquakes usually happen along faults, which are long cracks in the rock of the crust. Most faults are along the edges of tectonic plates. Earthquakes happen when blocks of rock on either side of a fault are moving past each other–and get stuck.

Shaking the ground

When moving blocks of rock get caught on each other, this causes pressure to build up. Suddenly, the rocks break free–and slip past each other. The pent-up energy is released as waves, called seismic waves, that make the ground shake. "Seismic" comes from the ancient Greek word for earthquake. After the main earthquake, smaller earthquakes, known as aftershocks, may follow over days or months.

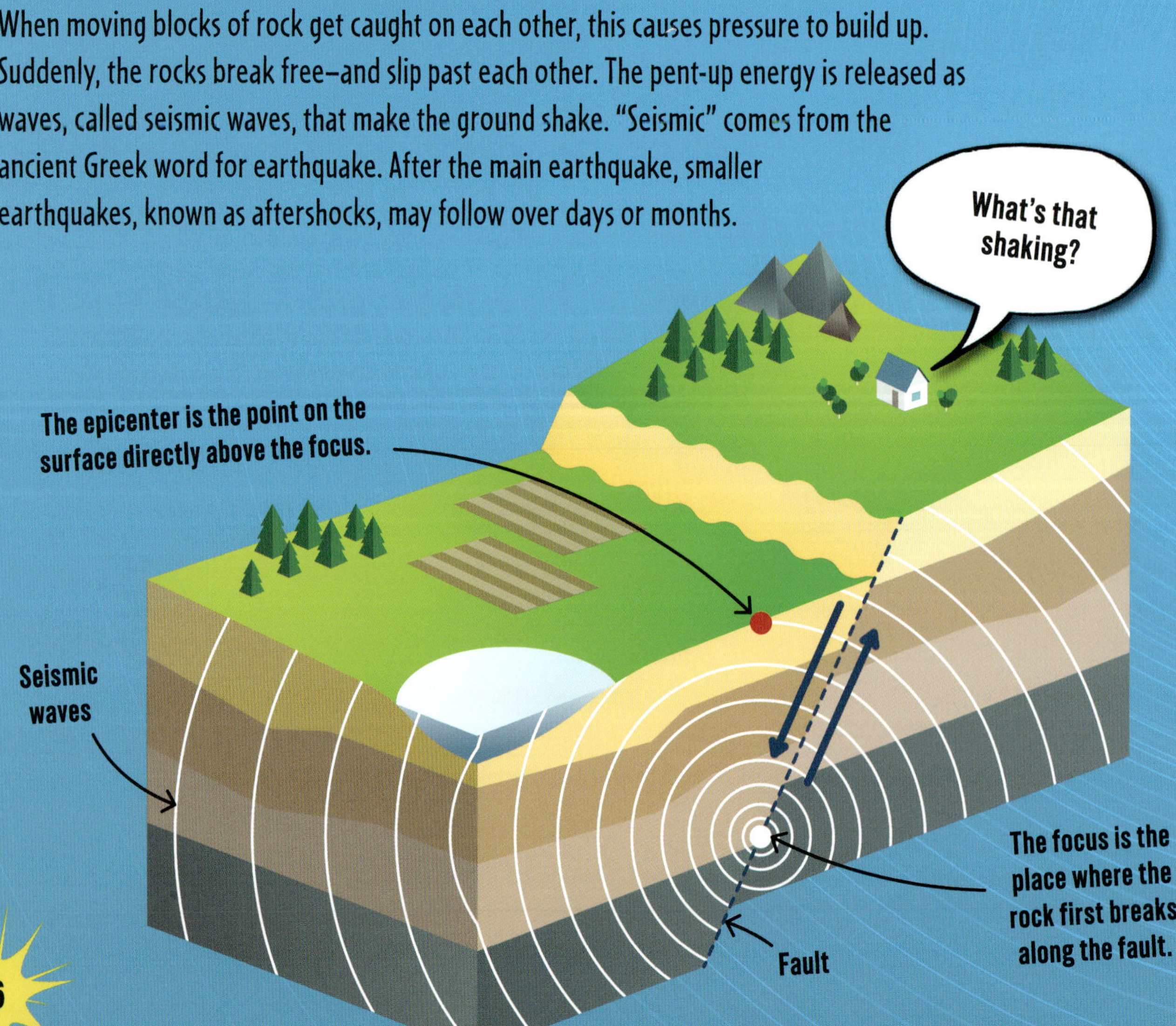

Create your own earthquake!

You will need a tray, two long pieces of cloth, soil, and sugar cubes. Check with an adult before you do this activity. Make sure you wash your hands carefully afterwards.

1. Lay your cloths flat in the tray so they are touching each other along one side. Make sure the ends of the cloths extend outside the tray. These cloths are the rocks on either side of a fault. You will pull the cloths to make an earthquake.

2. Cover the cloths in soil.

3. Build sugar cube houses on the soil.

4. Now make an earthquake by pulling the cloths in opposite directions. Tectonic plates do not move far: it is a sudden short movement that makes an earthquake.

5. What happens to your sugar cube houses?

Tray

Two long pieces of cloth

Soil

Sugar cubes

QUICK QUIZ!

In the southwestern United States, the San Andreas Fault can be seen aboveground (pictured on the left). The fault runs along the boundary between two large plates. Turn back to page 5 to figure out which plates.

MEASURING EARTHQUAKES

Seismologists are scientists who measure earthquakes.

Seismologists study earthquakes as well as the structure of Earth and its tectonic plates. They examine how plate movements can lead to powerful earthquakes.

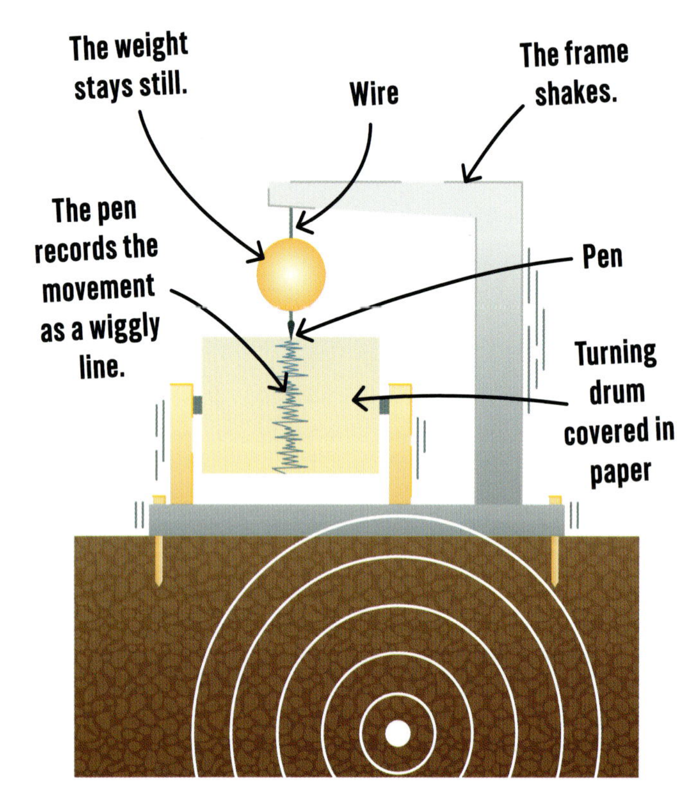

Sensitive seismographs

Seismologists use instruments called seismographs to measure the ground's shaking. A basic seismograph is fixed to the ground so that, when the ground shakes, the seismograph's frame shakes. However, a weight dangling from the frame does not shake. A pen records the difference in movement between the weight and the frame.

1 Can be felt only by a seismograph

2–3 Objects may shake

4 Objects may fall

Does anyone have any glue?

Scale of strength

The strength of earthquakes is measured on the moment magnitude scale. "Moment" is a measure of an earthquake's energy, while "magnitude" means size. The scale runs from 1 to 10, with each number equal to 32 times the power of the number before. Every day, there are hundreds of earthquakes of magnitude 1 or 2. Earthquakes of magnitude 8 and above happen only around once a year.

8–10 Cities near the epicenter may be destroyed

7 Buildings may collapse

5–6 Buildings may be damaged

Located on the Ring of Fire, Japan records around 2,000 earthquakes a year.

Did you know?

Ninety percent of earthquakes take place in a region called the Ring of Fire, around the edges of the Pacific Plate (see page 5).

TSUNAMIS

A tsunami is a series of huge ocean waves.

Tsunamis are very dangerous, but they are also very unusual. These giant waves are set off by an earthquake or eruption under the ocean. "Tsunami" means "harbor wave" in Japanese.

Growing waves

An undersea earthquake can disturb ocean water, making waves that spread out from the epicenter. As the waves travel across the ocean, they grow in height. After a tsunami hits the shore, the waves may travel miles inland if the ground is flat, which is why it is important to move to high ground during a tsunami. There may be five minutes to two hours between each wave of a tsunami.

As a tsunami approaches, the ocean may draw far out.

The approaching waves may make a roaring noise.

An earthquake sets off a tsunami.

The 2004 tsunami damaged the city of Banda Aceh, in Indonesia.

It's a fact

With a magnitude of 9.1–9.3, the most powerful earthquake of the 21st century took place on December 26, 2004, with its epicenter beneath the Indian Ocean. It set off tsunami waves up to 100 feet (30 m) high.

QUICK QUIZ!

Which of these is NOT a warning sign that a tsunami is on the way?

1. The ocean drawing unusually far out, exposing the seafloor.
2. A large rainbow in the sky.
3. The ocean making a loud roar, like an airplane engine.

EARTHQUAKE SAFETY

Seismologists help us to stay safe in earthquakes.

Seismologists try to give warnings of powerful earthquakes. In places where earthquakes are common, children are taught how to stay safe. People are encouraged to make their buildings extra strong.

Stay safe!

In an earthquake, drop to your hands and knees so you do not fall down. Take cover under a strong table or protect your head and neck with your arms. Hold on to your shelter until the shaking stops. Stay away from anything that could break or fall.

Build strong!

Earthquakes shake buildings from side to side. Earthquake-proof buildings need a strong but flexible frame, made of materials such as steel that bend without breaking. Some earthquake-proof buildings have flexible foundations (belowground parts), so only the building's base moves while the structure remains steady.

An ordinary building sways side to side in an earthquake.

A building with flexible foundations stays steady.

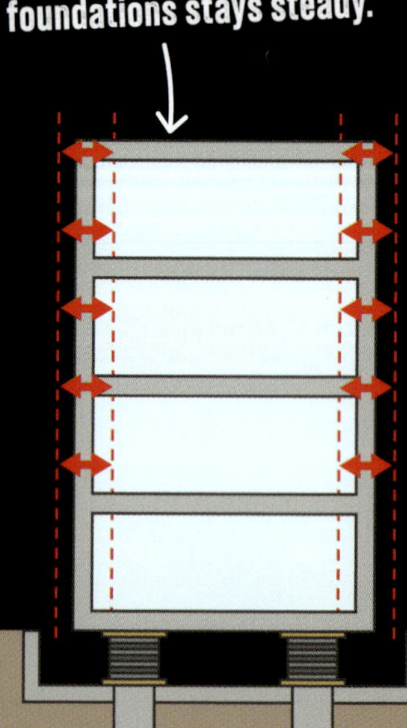

BE CAREFUL!

Toothpicks are sharp! If you are allergic to any of the ingredients in marshmallows, use modeling clay instead.

Construct an earthquake-proof building.

You will need a tray, Jell-O (or other gelatin dessert), toothpicks, and marshmallows.

1. Ask an adult to make Jell-O and pour it into your tray. Leave it in the fridge to set.

2. Use eight toothpicks and four marshmallows to construct a simple building. Use four upright toothpicks for the four corners of your building, sticking a marshmallow at the top of each. Then add four horizontal toothpicks in a square around the top.

3. Press your building into the Jell-O, then shake the tray. Does your building collapse?

4. How could you strengthen your building's frame by adding more toothpicks and more marshmallows?

5. Give your Jell-O a shake. What happens to your building now?

Jell-O

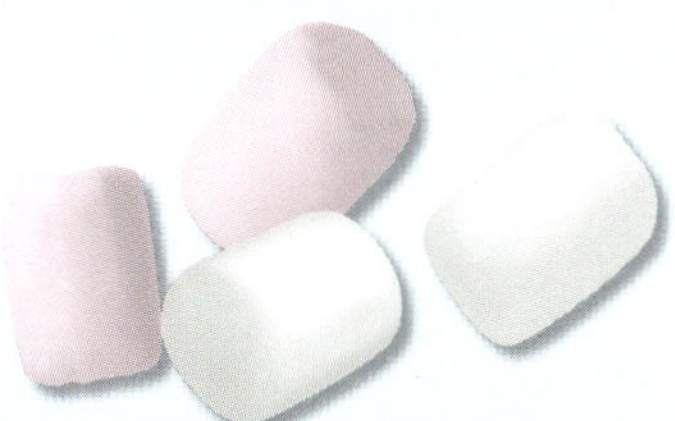

Marshmallows

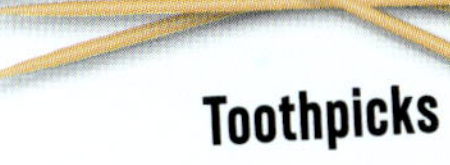

Toothpicks

Tray

WHAT MAKES A VOLCANO?

A volcano is an opening in Earth's crust where melted rock can escape.

Most volcanoes on land are found where tectonic plates are moving together, with one plate being pushed under the other. Beneath the oceans, many volcanoes are found where plates are moving apart.

A volcano is born

Where one plate is moving under another, rock melts. The melted rock, called magma, collects in an underground space called a magma chamber. When enough magma is in the chamber, it flows to the surface in an eruption. After it has erupted, magma is called lava.

Where plates are moving apart, magma from the mantle rushes up to fill the crack, making volcanoes. Volcanoes can also form in the middle of plates over super-hot areas of the mantle called hot spots.

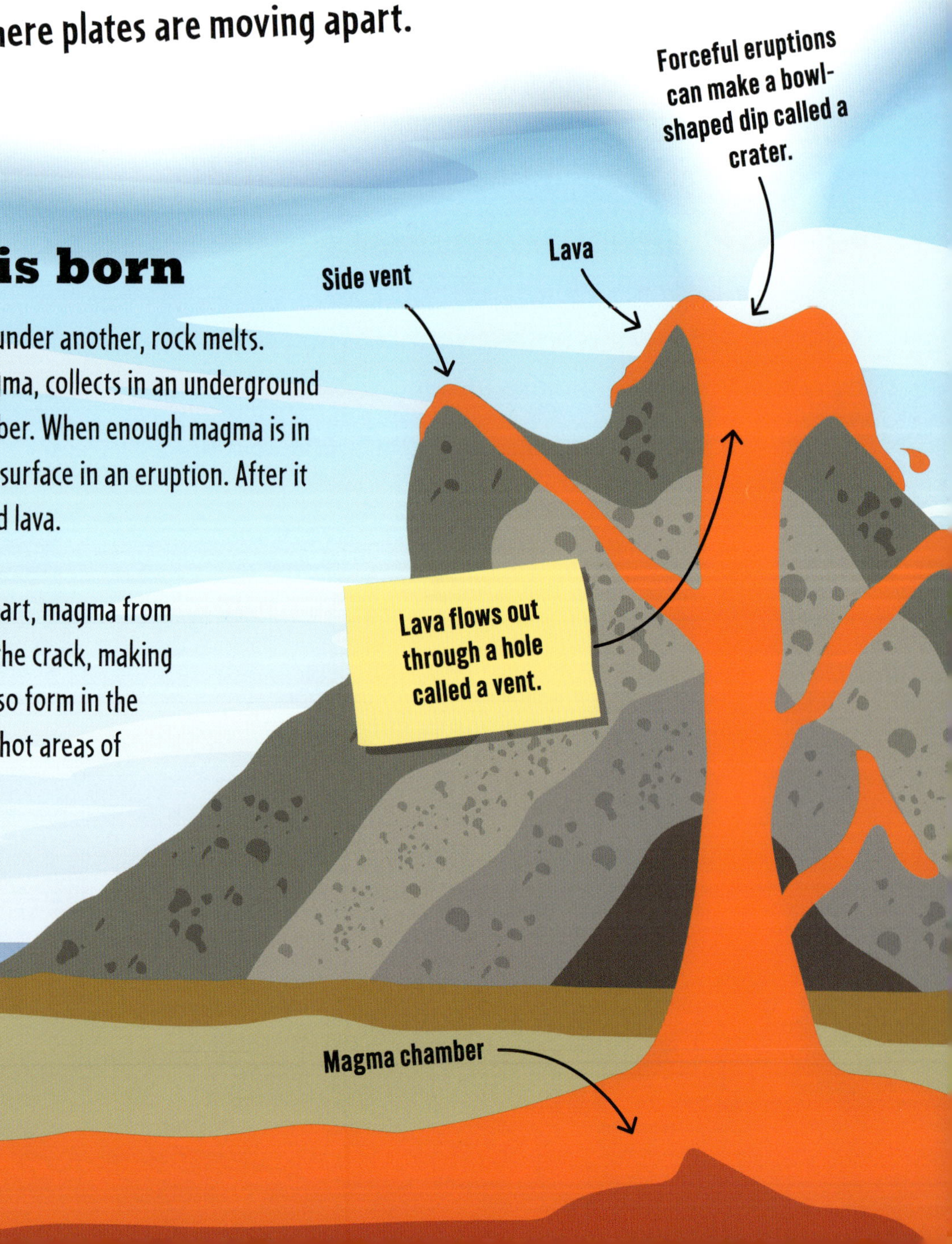

Forceful eruptions can make a bowl-shaped dip called a crater.

Lava

Side vent

Lava flows out through a hole called a vent.

Magma chamber

PHOTO QUIZ!
Which one of these volcanoes formed over a hot spot?
1
The United States' Mount St. Helens formed where the small Juan de Fuca Plate is moving beneath the North American Plate.
2
Mount Kilimanjaro, in Tanzania, is the tallest mountain in Africa. It formed as lava welled to the surface where the African Plate is splitting into two.
What volcano?
Over time, cooled lava can build a volcano into a mountain.
3
This volcano, named Kīlauea, is on the Big Island of Hawaii in the middle of the Pacific Plate. Around 100,000 years ago, it became tall enough to be seen above the ocean surface.

VOLCANO SHAPES

Volcanoes are many shapes and sizes.

A volcano's appearance depends on how it formed. It also depends on the runniness of the lava that flows from the volcano—and how far it flows before cooling into solid rock.

Volcano types

STRATOVOLCANO

Stratovolcanoes often form where one tectonic plate is moving under another. Their lava is thick, so it does not flow far before it cools into solid rock. Layers of cooled lava and ash build up a cone-shaped mountain with steep sides.

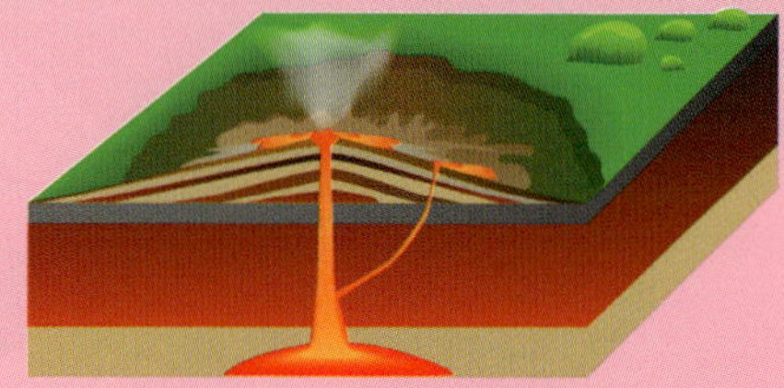

SHIELD VOLCANO

These volcanoes often form over hot spots or where plates are moving apart. Their lava is thin and runny, so it flows a long way before hardening. This builds a low volcano, a little like a warrior's shield lying on the ground.

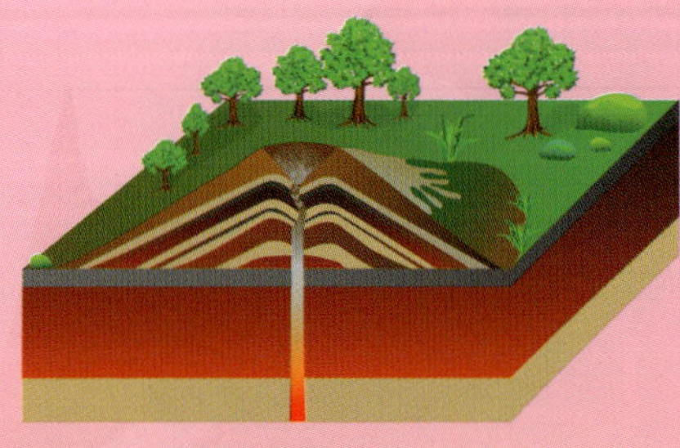

LAVA DOME

Dome-shaped volcanoes are built by slow eruptions of very thick lava. This creates a rounded mound of hardened lava. Lava domes are found where plates are moving together.

FISSURE VENT

Fissure vents are long cracks in the ground, through which lava flows. Fissure vents do not usually build up into a mountain or mound. They are found where plates are moving apart.

BE CAREFUL!
Check the ingredients of your "lavas" in case you are allergic.

Find out how different "lavas" flow!

You will need a tray, a cutting board, something to prop up the board on, paper, tape, a stopwatch, a spoon, oil, runny honey, and ketchup. Check with an adult before you do this activity.

1. A liquid's thickness is known as its viscosity. To investigate how lavas flow, we will experiment with liquids of different viscosities: oil, honey, and ketchup.

2. Stick the paper to your cutting board, then prop up the cutting board inside the tray so one end is higher than the other, like the side of a volcano.

3. Take a spoonful of your first liquid, oil, then pour it at the top of your chopping board. Time how long it takes the oil to reach the bottom of the paper. Examine your paper.

4. Change your paper, then repeat step 3 with the honey and the ketchup.

5. Which liquid flows most slowly? Which liquid behaves like the lava that forms stratovolcanoes and which behaves like the lava that forms shield volcanoes?

ERUPTIONS

A volcano can erupt lava, gas, ash, or chunks of rock.

A volcano erupts when its magma chamber is filled with magma or bubbles with gas. Different volcanoes have different types of eruptions. Some are fast and violent, while others are slow and steady.

Eruption types

Types of eruptions are named after famous volcanoes that erupt in that way. The strength of eruptions is measured on the volcanic explosivity index (VEI), which runs from 0 up to 8. Undersea eruptions are the most common, but they are usually less explosive than aboveground eruptions because of the weight of the cooling water.

Hawaiian eruptions (VEI 0–1) are the calmest, with flows of runny lava that contain little gas.

These eruptions (VEI 1–2) are of lava that bubbles with gas, throwing lava high into the air.

Vulcanian eruptions (VEI 2–4) are of thick, gassy lava, which is hurled into the air and can land as solid chunks called lava bombs.

These explosive eruptions (VEI 4) result from the collapse of a lava dome. Hot gas, ash, and lava chunks surge down the volcano's slopes in what is known as a pyroclastic flow.

Plinian eruptions (VEI 5–7) are extremely explosive and long-lasting, with ash thrown up to 28 miles (45 km) into the air and pyroclastic flows that travel downhill at up to 435 miles (700 km) per hour.

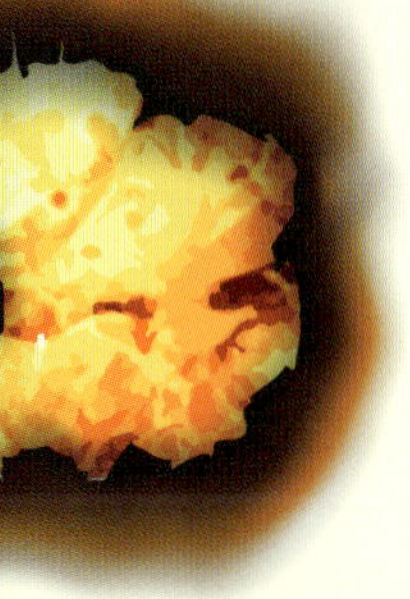

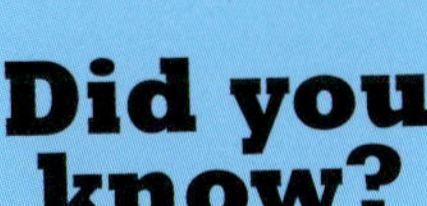

In 79 CE, a Plinian eruption of Mount Vesuvius, in Italy, created pyroclastic flows that killed at least 1,500 people. The Roman cities of Pompeii and Herculaneum were buried in ash.

Victims of the Mount Vesuvius eruption were covered by ash, which hardened and left hollows where their bodies had been. The hollows have now been filled with plaster, so we can see the shapes of the victims.

SUPERVOLCANOES

Supervolcanoes are super big, but they do not erupt often!

A supervolcano is a volcano with eruptions that measure 8 on the volcanic explosivity index (see page 18). A supervolcano eruption can cover hundreds of miles with lava and ash.

A supervolcano may look like nothing more than a large dip in the ground. This is Long Valley Caldera in California.

UNITED STATES

SOUTH AMERICA

Where are supervolcanoes?

Only about 13 of the world's volcanoes are supervolcanoes. These form when magma is unable to break through the crust so it builds an immense magma chamber–until finally the pressure is so great that it bursts out! The eruption leaves behind a vast hollow in the ground, called a caldera. A supervolcano usually goes tens of thousands of years between eruptions.

PHOTO QUIZ!

This photo shows the Toba supervolcano in Indonesia. Its last eruption, 70,000 years ago, left a wide hollow that filled with water. What is the scientific name for that hollow: calculator, caldera, or calorie?

The most recent supervolcano eruption took place 28,500 years ago. The Taupō Volcano, in New Zealand, released 280 cubic miles (1,170 cu km) of lava, rock, and ash.

NEW ZEALAND

ACTIVE OR EXTINCT?

Volcanoes are active, dormant, or extinct.

An active volcano is erupting now or likely to erupt again. An extinct volcano will not erupt again because it no longer has a supply of magma beneath it. A dormant volcano has not erupted for thousands of years, but might erupt again.

Moving along

The islands of Hawaii in the Pacific Ocean formed over a hot spot in the mantle (see page 14). As the tectonic plate above the hot spot moved slowly along, one volcano formed over the hot spot after another, making a line of volcanoes. The volcanoes grew above sea level, making the Hawaiian Islands.

As the tectonic plate continued to move, each volcano was moved away from the hot spot and became extinct as a new, active volcano formed!

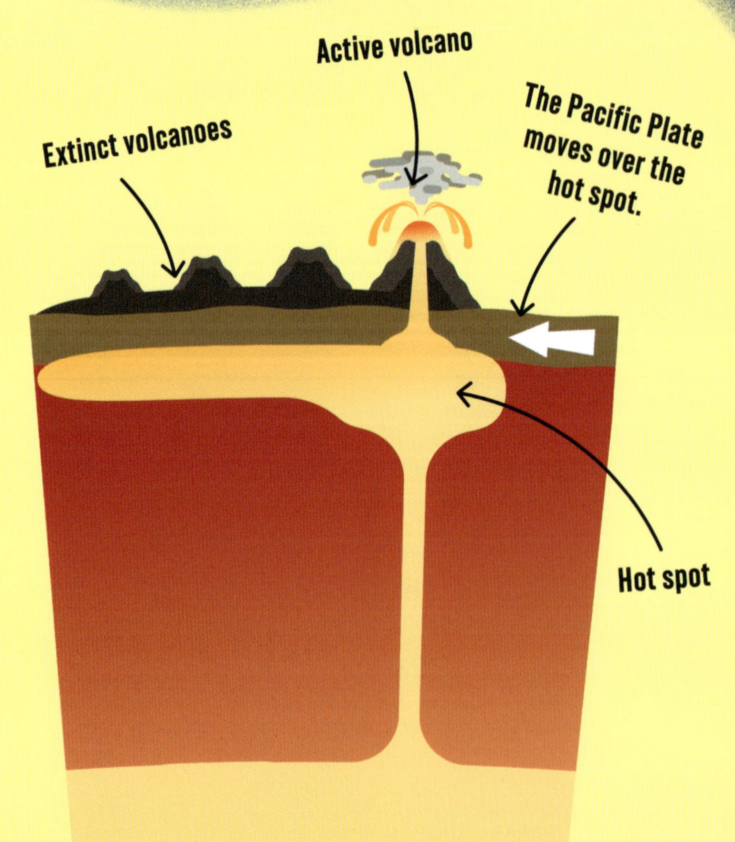

It's a fact

Until 2006, Fourpeaked Volcano in Alaska was thought to be extinct because it had not erupted for 10,000 years. Then it erupted!

PHOTO QUIZ!

One of these volcanoes is active, one is dormant and one is extinct. Which is which?

HOT SPRINGS AND GEYSERS

These hot water features are found near volcanoes.

A hot spring is where water heated by magma flows to Earth's surface. A fumarole is an opening in the ground from which steam bursts. Rarest and most exciting of all is a geyser, which is a hole that sprays water and steam.

Super sprays

All these features form over magma chambers, where water from rain has soaked into the ground. Geysers form when water flows down through a tubelike hole in the rock to around 6,500 feet (2,000 m) deep, where it is heated by hot rocks. The water boils and bubbles. When the pressure becomes too much, the water and steam rush to the surface. After the tube has refilled with water, the geyser erupts again.

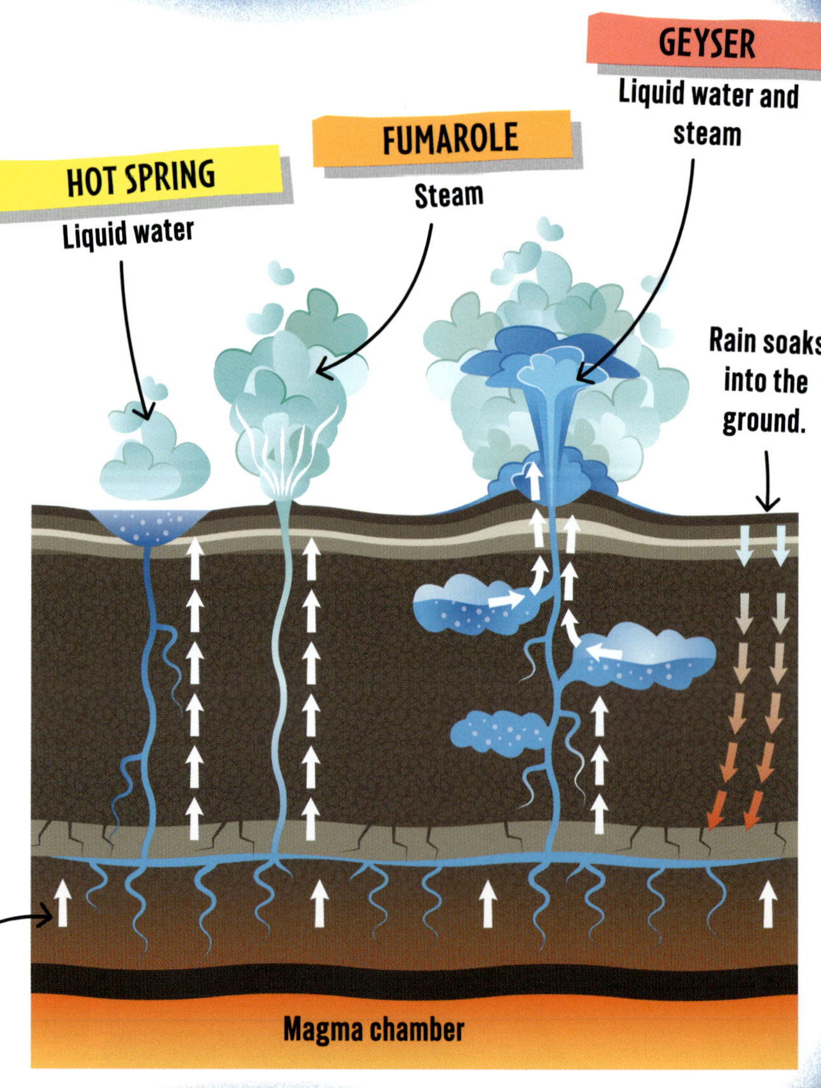

In Yellowstone National Park, the Grand Prismatic Spring's bright colors are caused by bacteria that live in the hot water.

Did you know?

More than half the world's geysers and hot springs are in Yellowstone National Park, which is in the caldera of the dormant Yellowstone Supervolcano.

Yellowstone's Old Faithful geyser erupts at least once every two hours.

LIVING WITH VOLCANOES

Volcanoes are both dangerous and helpful.

Living close to an active volcano seems risky, but there are farms, towns, and even cities around volcanoes. That is because volcanoes bring many benefits!

BENEFITS

Fertile soil

Lava and ash contain minerals that enrich the soil, making healthy crops.

Geothermal energy

The heat of magma ("geothermal" means "earth heat") can be used to boil water to form steam that turns turbine wheels to make electricity.

Relaxation

People and other animals, such as these Japanese macaques, enjoy hot springs.

Materials

The rock that forms when lava cools can be used for buildings or carvings, such as these statues on Easter Island in the Pacific Ocean.

DANGERS

Lava flows

On steep slopes, lava can flow downhill at up to 6.2 miles (10 km) per hour.

Ash in the air

Volcanic ash can irritate the eyes and lungs, and is not safe for airplanes to fly through.

Hot gas

Pyroclastic flows can reach 1,300°F (700°C), melting metal and starting fires.

Landslides

Eruptions can set off landslides when rocks, mud, or trees fall downhill.

It's a fact

Iceland has around 130 volcanoes, which heat water that is piped to 90 percent of the country's homes to keep them warm.

QUICK QUIZ ANSWERS

PAGE 5

1 inch
(3 cm)

PAGE 7

The San Andreas Fault runs for around 745 miles (1,200 km) along the transform boundary between the Pacific Plate and the North American Plate. Movement along the fault causes frequent earthquakes, including the 1906 San Francisco earthquake.

PAGE 11

2. A large rainbow is not a sign that a tsunami is on its way. Both 1 and 3 are signs of an approaching tsunami: the ocean drawing unusually far out and the ocean making a loud roar. In coastal areas where earthquakes are common, there may also be warning sirens or announcements on the Internet and television. If you believe a tsunami is on the way, get to high ground as far inland as possible. There may be signs telling you which way to go.

PAGE 15

3. Kīlauea formed over a hot spot in the middle of the Pacific Plate.

PAGE 21

Caldera

PAGE 23

1. Mount Etna is active: it erupts almost constantly.
2. Castle Rock is extinct: it has not erupted for millions of years, so it is completely safe to live on!
3. Mauna Kea is dormant: it has not erupted for 4,000 to 6,000 years, so scientists have risked building observatories for watching the stars on its slopes.

NOW TEST YOUR KNOWLEDGE!

1 **How hot is Earth's core?**

a. 140°F (60°C)

b. 1,110°F (600°C)

c. 10,800°F (6,000°C)

2 **What is the name for a scientist who studies earthquakes?**

a. Oceanographer

b. Seismologist

c. Zoologist

3 **During an earthquake, where should you take cover?**

a. Under a strong table

b. Under a blanket

c. Under a tree

4 **What is the name for magma that has erupted from a volcano?**

a. Loofah

b. Lather

c. Lava

5 **Around how many supervolcanoes are there?**

a. 13

b. 130

c. 1,300

6 **How often does the Old Faithful geyser erupt?**

a. Around once every two years.

b. Around once every two days.

c. Around once every two hours.

ANSWERS ON PAGE 31

GLOSSARY

bacteria - tiny, simple living things

caldera - a large hollow in the ground made by a volcanic eruption

core - Earth's innermost layer, made of super-hot metal

crust - Earth's outer layer, made of solid rock

earthquake - shaking of the ground, usually caused by the movement of tectonic plates

earthquake-proof - able to stand an earthquake

epicenter - the point on Earth's surface above the starting point of an earthquake

eruption - when lava, gas, ash, and rock are released from a volcano

fault - a long crack in Earth's crust, formed by the movement of tectonic plates

flexible - able to bend

hot spot - an area where the mantle is particularly hot

lava - melted rock that is above Earth's surface

magma - melted rock that is beneath Earth's surface

magma chamber - an underground space where melted rock collects

mantle - the layer of Earth between the core and the crust, made of rock that is partly melted

mineral - a solid that forms in the ground or in water

molten - made liquid by heat

pyroclastic flow - a mass of hot gas, lava chunks, and ash that flows from a volcano

rock - a solid that is a mixture of minerals

seismologist - a scientist who studies earthquakes and Earth's structure

stabilize - to make less likely to collapse or overturn

steam - a white mist of tiny water droplets, made when water is heated

supervolcano - an unusually large volcano

tectonic plates - massive slabs of rock that form Earth's crust and upper mantle

turbine - a machine in which the movement of steam or another gas or liquid turns a wheel, which makes electricity

volcanic ash - tiny bits of rock

volcano - a hole in Earth's crust through which hot, liquid rock can escape

FURTHER READING

BOOKS

Andrews, Elizabeth. *Why Do Volcanoes Erupt?* Minneapolis, MN: Pop!, a division of Abdo, 2022.

Beckerman, Nell Cross. *Volcanoes*. New York, NY: Scholastic, 2024.

Jackson, Tom. *Volcanoes & Earthquakes*. New York, NY: DK Publishing, 2023.

WEBSITES

www.earthquakeauthority.com/Blog/2020/San-Andreas-Fault-Line-Map
Discover more about the United States' San Andreas Fault.

kids.nationalgeographic.com/science/article/volcano
Read even more fun facts about volcanoes here.

www.nhm.ac.uk/discover/how-to-make-a-volcano.html
Follow the Natural History Museum's guide to making your own volcano.

Answers: 1c, 2b, 3a, 4c, 5a, 6c

INDEX